SPORTS ENCYCLOPEDIA

WINTER AND MISCELLANEOUS SPORTS

Om KIDZ
An imprint of Om Books International

Contents

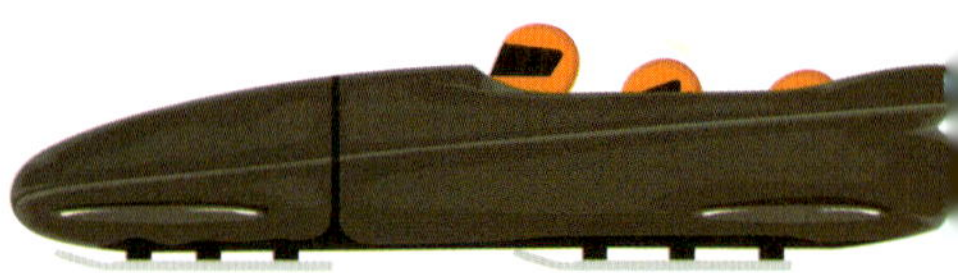

WINTER SPORTS

Winter sports are those sports which are primarily played in a low temperature environment. Most of these sports are variations of skiing, ice skating and sledding.

Traditionally, winter sports were played in cold areas during the winter season only, but artificial snow and ice allow more flexibility to the players. Also, it allows the players to practice during off-season months. Thus, winter sports can be played indoors or outdoors, depending on the climate. While many winter sports are for individuals, there are several that can be played in teams. Some winter sports are time based, where the emphasis is on speed. Whereas others take into account the team skills and tactics used against another team, or individual in the running.

The beauty of winter sports is that they help get rid of the excess lethargy and shivers that might accompany the biting cold. Winter sports have gained so much popularity that they have a separate section of games in the Olympics called "Winter Olympics".

Let's get ready to glide through these sports!

Did you know? It is not compulsory that all countries participate in the Olympics. However, UK, USA, France, Italy, Austria, Canada, Finland and Hungary have faithfully sent players to the Winter Olympics every year.

Ice Hockey

Ice hockey is one of the most popular winter sports. It is a contact sport similar to hockey, but it is played in an ice rink. It is a part of the Winter Olympics. It is also the national sport of Canada.

Origin

Stick-and-ball games have been played by people for centuries. They were especially popular in Europe. The old Irish game called "hurling" was very similar to field hockey. In places that used to experience regular snowfall, this game was adapted to play on ice.

When the British soldiers went to Canada, they took the stick-and-ball games with them. Canada would experience snow and ice during winter. They played these games on the ice. John Franklin once called "the game of hockey played on ice" as a morning sport for his friends and himself. They would play this sport during their Arctic expeditions on the Great Bear Lake.

In 1835, US folk artist John Toole painted skaters with long sticks playing on frozen ice. Canada's folk tales describe people playing ice hockey, but at the time, this game was called "hurleys". School boys in Canadian boarding schools and colleges played the sport and called it "hurly on ice". It is from Canada that the game of ice hockey evolved into what it is today.

Players wear heavily padded shirts and shorts for safety.

Ice hockey players must wear helmets. It is an important safety precaution to prevent injury during a fall.

The skates used in ice hockey are optimised to increase the speed, movement and comfort of the player, as players need to make quick turns and stops.

Rules

Hockey and ice hockey have similar rules and objectives. However, the exact rules depend on the code of play being used. The two most important codes are those of the International Ice Hockey Federation (IIHF) and the Canadian-founded and North American-expanded National Hockey League (NHL). Both codes originated from the Canadian rules of ice hockey, which were created in the early twentieth century.

Ice hockey is played on a hockey rink. During normal play, there are six players from each side on the ice at any given time. One of the players is the goaltender. All players wear ice skates.

The objective of the game is to score goals by shooting the puck (a hard and durable rubber disc) into the opponent's goal net. The players control the puck using a hockey stick.

The five players are divided into three forwards and two defencemen. The forward positions consist of a centre and two wingers: a left wing and a right wing. The defencemen usually stay together as a pair, generally divided between left and right.

There are three major rules of play in ice hockey that limit the movement of the puck. These are called "offside", "icing" and the puck going out of play. A player is "offside" if he/she enters his/her opponent's zone before the puck itself. The puck goes "out of play" whenever it goes past the perimeter of the ice rink.

The blue lines divide the rink into three zones—offensive zone, neutral zone and defending zone.

The neutral zone trap is designed to isolate the puck carrier in the neutral zone, preventing him/her from entering the offensive zone.

The circles show the positions of the right and left defencemen.

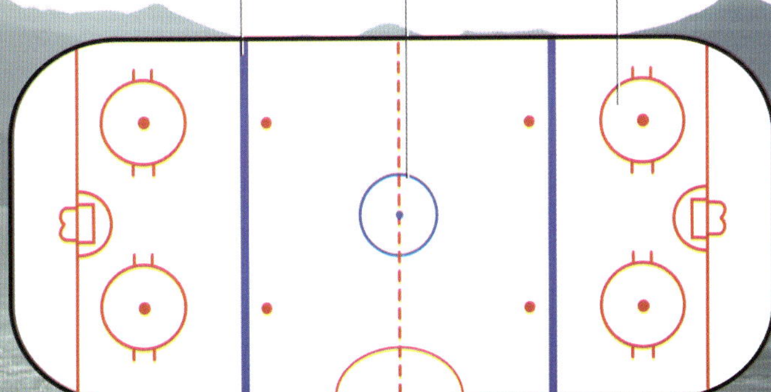

Wall of fame

Hayley Wickenheiser plays for Canada. Her team has won four golds and one silver at the Winter Olympics ice hockey competitions.

Soviet Union's Vladislav Tretiak is considered to be one of the greatest goaltenders in the sport of ice hockey.

Igor Kravchuk from the Soviet Union won a gold medal at the Calgary and the Albertville games.

Fact card

- Ice hockey has been named as the fastest game on Earth.
- Goaltenders wear different equipment from the rest of the team as the hockey pucks travel towards them at a speed greater than 100 mph. They wear greater protection. Their uniforms have more padding, their leg pads are much larger and their gloves are padded enough to catch or block pucks.
- The skates worn by goaltenders are optimised for faster and sudden movements.

Bandy

Bandy is a winter sport which is played on ice. The players wear skates and carry sticks. Instead of a puck, they try to put a small ball into the opponent team's goal. Bandy is the second-most popular winter sport after ice hockey. The Federation of International Bandy regulates the sport around the world.

During an ongoing match, the defending team hopes to gain possession of the ball.

Origin

There are records of the Russian monastery playing a game similar to bandy in the tenth and eleventh centuries. The modern version of this game was played back in eighteenth century Russia.

Much later, when this game travelled to parts of Europe and finally reached England, it was revamped with a new set of rules. Bandy is also called "Russian hockey", Russia holds a strong claim to this sport

Rules

There are 18 rules in official play. The same rules apply to all levels of bandy, although certain alterations for junior, senior or female players are permitted. Each team consists of eight or 11 players depending on the platform. This number includes the goalkeeper. Only the goalkeepers can touch the ball with their hands. But this is only permitted within the penalty area of their own goal post.

Players are required to wear skates, a helmet, a mouth guard and, in the case of the goalkeeper, a face guard. Free-strokes can be awarded to a team if a player of the opposite team breaks a rule. A penalty shot is awarded if a defender violently attacks an opponent within the penalty area.

As seen in ice hockey, players of this sport must wear helmets for protection.

Players wear padded gloves to warm their hands and get a good grip on the stick. It also keeps their hands safe during a fall.

The bandy stick is similar to a hockey stick. It is also called a "bandy" and is curved at one end.

Fact card

- The name of this sport comes from the English phrase "to bandy" and from the French word "bander", which means "to strike back and forth".
- Before the name was changed, this sport was called "hockey on ice".

Curling

Curling is a fairly old winter sport. It is a fun and informal game in its most popular format, despite its Olympic status. The game is similar to skipping stones and works on similar physical principles.

Granite is used for making curling stones. It is heavy in size and is regularly polished for maintenance.

Origin

Curling is said to have originated in Scotland. It dates back to the sixteenth century. Originally, the stones were just flat-bottomed river stones which were of varied sizes, shapes and smoothness. This means that the players had little to no control over the curl or velocity of the stone. They had to rely more on luck rather than skill to play the game.

The word "curling" first appeared in print in 1620 in Scotland in a poem by Henry Adamson. Today, this game is most widely played in Canada.

Gameplay

Curling has been an official sport of the Winter Olympics Games since 1924.

- **Curling sheet** – It is a rectangular area of ice carefully prepared to be as flat and level as possible. The house consists of four concentric rings at the end of the sheet.
- **Curling stone** – It is made of granite and weighs between 17 and 20 kg, as specified by the World Curling Federation.
- **Curling broom** – It is used to sweep the ice surface in the path of the stone. It may be used for balancing during delivery of the stone.

The aim of the game is to score points by getting stones closer to the house centre, than the other team's stones. Players from either team take alternate shots. The game ends when the team delivers all eight shots. The winning team is the one with the highest score.

The curling sheet is made as flat and smooth as possible. It is completely made of ice. The borders of the sheet are called "backboards".

Several ice sheets are laid out together to make the playing area. This is to enable many players to play at one time.

The curling broom or brush is swept along the icy surface. The stone is pushed forward and backward so that it does not disturb the ice sheet.

Fact card

- This game needs lots of strategy and teamwork. For every move, the player needs to first think of the ideal position for the curling stone. The use of so much strategic thinking has given the sport the nickname of "chess on ice".
- Targets are drawn on the vertical ends of sheets. It is called the "house". A point is awarded to the team which manages to put the curling stone in the target.

Ice Yachting

"Ice yachting" is the name given to the sport in which people race sailboats or iceboats called "ice yachts". These boats have skis and runners fitted to them so that they can move on the surface of ice.

Origin

Interestingly, there is evidence of iceboating as early as 2000 BCE. The use of iceboats as a means of transport in winter dates back to the seventeenth and eighteenth centuries on the frozen Gulf of Riga and in the Netherlands.

The sport began in the mid-nineteenth century, and the Poughkeepsie Ice Yacht Club was formed in 1865. The ice yachts of the nineteenth century were huge and they were made of wood. They had six or seven crew members.

Modern iceboats can move at speeds of over 145 kmph. The design of the iceboats have aerodynamic features, which give low friction and high wind speed.

Ice yachting is practiced in countries like Germany, Great Britain, Poland, Sweden, Norway and Austria. It is most popular in the USA and Canada. Different countries use different designs of iceboats based on the extremity of weather conditions. Ice yachting was one of the biggest trends on the Hudson River in the 1790s.

This picture shows one of the older models of ice yachts.

Fact card

- Ice yachting was initially considered a symbol of wealth because very few could afford the equipment and the time spent in sailing.
- Ice yachting became less popular in Europe after World War II. It picked up popularity again once the design of the iceboats was improved and the speed of the iceboats increased greatly.

Rules

An iceboat is similar to a sailboat. Blades fixed to the bottom of the boat help it travel on ice. A vertical mast carries a sail which helps the boat move by harnessing the wind. The structures of modern iceboats are made of steel and the cockpits in their hulls can accommodate a crew. A steering runner is mounted near the hull and can be used by the helmsman.

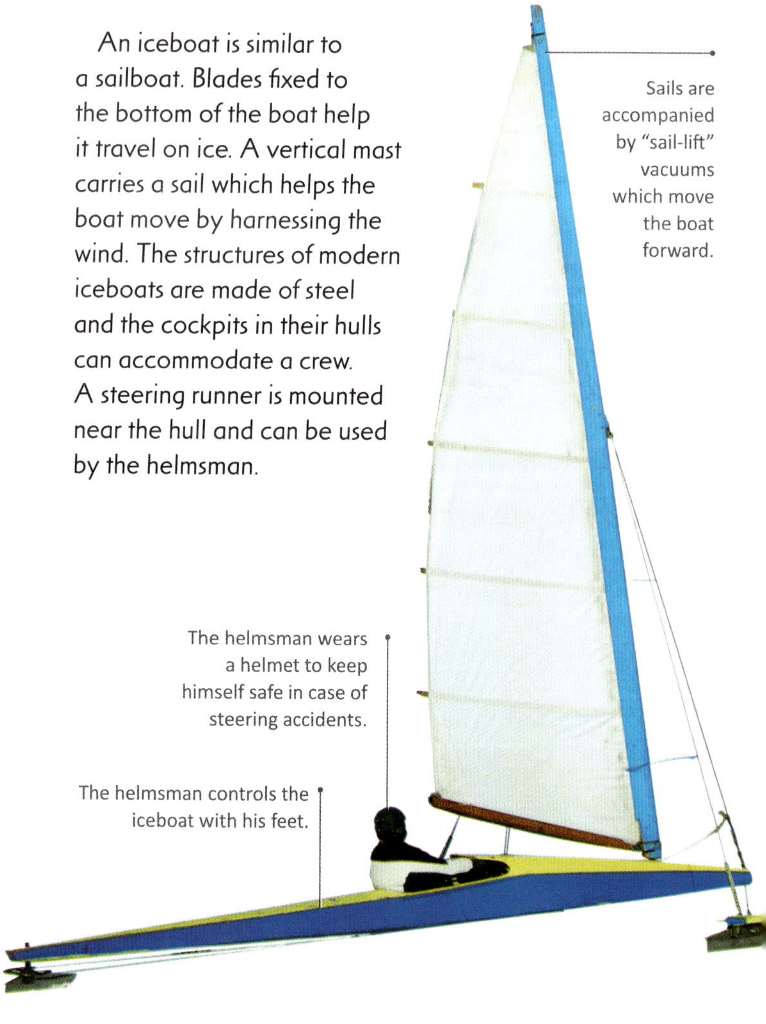

Sails are accompanied by "sail-lift" vacuums which move the boat forward.

The helmsman wears a helmet to keep himself safe in case of steering accidents.

The helmsman controls the iceboat with his feet.

Ringette

Ringette is a game that is almost completely confined to Canada. It is similar to hockey because it uses a stick and is played on skates. However, there are many key differences.

The goalie and the player wear different kinds of gloves. The goalie's gloves are heavily padded.

Origin

Ringette was invented in 1963 in North Bay, Ontario, Canada, by a man named Sam Jacks. It was originally designed to provide an alternate on-ice game for female athletes. But it eventually became a two-gender sport with emphasis on speed and team play.

Ringette is an exciting, fast-paced non-contact sport. It is played on ice with skates and sticks. There are two teams, each team has six players (five skaters and one goalie).

Rules

The aim of the game is to score goals. This is achieved by shooting the object of play into nets placed at either side of the rink. The equipment used to play ringette includes skates, a straight stick with a specially designed tip to pass and shoot and a blue rubber ring.

Players wear gloves, elbow pads, knee pads, shin pads, long padded pants, a helmet with a triangular spaced face mask (to prevent the bladeless ringette stick from penetrating the helmet), a neck guard and a jersey.

The emphasis is on team spirit and the skating skills of the team. Players cannot carry the ring across the blue lines on ice. Only three players from each team, plus the defending goalie, are allowed in the end zones at the same time, which keeps the play open.

This is the goal area. The goalie cannot touch the ring outside the blue area with the red border.

Fact card

- Ringette was originally meant to be a women-only sport.

There is a shot clock which starts when a team gains possession of the ring. If they have not taken a shot on the net within 30 seconds, a horn sounds and the ring is then awarded to the opposing team.

The end of the stick is put within the hole of the ring and controlled in this way.

Figure Skating

Figure skating focusses on form, balance and grace.

Figure skating is an ice skating sport. Many consider it to be the winter sport equivalent of gymnastics. Figure skating focusses heavily on grace and dance-like movements.

Origin

An Englishman named Robert Jones was apparently the first person to mention figure skating in his book "A Treatise on Skating" in 1772. The style of this sport was very strict and formal back then. It was not at all like the modern figure skating we know today.

Jackson Haines introduced a new style of skating in the mid-1860s and it is now considered to be the international style. His style was free and expressive. It was based on imitating dance moves on skates. Haines is known as the "father of modern figure skating". Although his style was picked up in Europe, it did not catch on in the USA until after his death.

The International Skating Union was founded in 1892. The first European Championships were held in 1891 and the first World Championships were held in 1896. Pair skating was introduced at the 1908 World Championships, where the title was won by Anna Hubler and Heinrich Burger. Figure skating was first introduced in the Olympics in1908.

Figure skaters wear costumes that have sequins. They are form-fitting performance costumes.

Figure skating is similar to synchronised swimming; it can be performed as a solo act, in pairs or in groups.

Figure skates have boots and sharp blades that are attached with screws to the sole of the boot.

Rules

Following are the rules and regulations for the skates that are used by figure skaters.

The figure skates have a set of large, jagged teeth called toe picks or toe rakes on the front of the blade. The toe picks are used primarily in jumping.

Blades are mounted to the sole and heel of the boot with screws. When viewed from the side, the blade of a figure skate is not flat, but curved slightly. This curve is also known as the "rocker of the blade".

Beneath the ball of the foot is, what is known as, the "sweet spot" of the blade which is very essential for performing spins. The blade itself is hollow. A groove on the bottom of the blade creates two distinct edges inside and outside the blade.

Skating rink:

Dimensions of ice rinks vary with the associations. The rink dimension for Olympic or International Ice Hockey is 30 m × 60 m (98.5 feet × 197 feet). The rink dimension for the National Hockey League is 26 m × 61 m (85 feet × 200 feet). The European rinks are usually 30 m × 64 m (98.5 feet × 210 feet).

Olympic-sized rinks are usually chosen by the International Skating Union for figure skating competitions, especially for major events.

This skater is rotating on one foot to perform a spin move. Spins can be done on the floor and during a jump move.

Dance moves:

- **Jumps** - During a jump move, the skater leaps into the air and quickly rotates to land back on the ice after completing one or more rotations. Each jump is given a score. Toe jumps, loop jumps and axel are a few types of jumps.
- **Spins** - During a spin, the skater rotates on the round part of the blade called the "front rocker". Spins are a required element in the Olympic sports. There are three types of spins; camel, sit, and upright spin.
- **Lifts** - Lifts are required elements in ice dancing and pair skating. Judges observe the speed, ice coverage, leg position, body's stability and cleanliness while scoring.

Blades are made of carbon steel, which is coated with high-quality chrome.

Wall of fame

Female Olympic figure skating champion Adelina Sotnikova won a gold medal in 2014.

Kim Yuna, a South Korean figure skater, won a silver medal.

Carolina Kostner from Italy won the bronze medal in figure skating.

Fact card

- Earlier, only men competed in these events. In 1902, a woman, Madge Syers, entered the World Competition for the first time and finished in the second place. The ISU quickly banned women from competing against men. They established a separate competition for women in 1906.
- In its first years, ice dance was dominated by British skaters. Beginning with Jean Westwood and Lawrence Demmy, British couples won the world title every year through the 1960s.
- Many movies have been inspired by the sport of figure skating and have been based on themes of the same. *On Thin Ice* is one such movie.
- Figure skating is one of the oldest sports to be on the Winter Olympics programme.

Short-Track Speed Skating

Short-track speed racing is a multiplayer sport. Ice skaters race against each other in this sport.

Take a look at the lines made on the ice by the skaters. The ice rinks need to be regularly cleaned and maintained to keep the floor smooth.

Origin

Short-track speed skating first began in the speed skating events. This was mainly practiced in the USA and Canada.

At the Winter Olympics in 1932, speed skating events were among the mass start competitions.

1967 saw track speed skating included as an international sport by the International Skating Union. However, they did not hold any international competitions until 1976. Since 1981, World Championships have been held.

Gameplay

Short-track skating is a sport played against other competitors and not against time. Four to eight racers skate in a group and compete on an indoor track the size of a hockey rink. They take laps and the length of each lap is 111 m. The top two finishers from each round proceed to the next round. Ice skaters make sharp turns at high speeds. Therefore, they use a special type of skates which gives them speed. The skates have a taller blade and higher boot, which provide extra support to the skater. Skaters wear protective pads on their elbows and knees. They also wear helmets and gloves.

The ice skaters use a special type of skates which allow quick movement.

Fact card

- At the 1988 Winter Olympics in Canada, short track was a demonstration sport. It was upgraded to a full Olympic sport in 1992.

Types of races

Individual short-track races are held over a distance of 500, 1000, 1500 and 3000 m for both men and women.

Four-person relay races cover distances of 3000 m (for women) and 5000 m (for men).

Violations & penalties

A skater is given a penalty from a race if any of their actions are considered to be violations. In such a case, their time is written off as "invalid".

Penalties are given to skaters if:

- a skater is pushing, blocking, tripping or coming between another skater
- a skater moves outside his/her designated track
- a team or an individual sets up the result of the competition
- a skater assists another skater physically by pushing him/her from behind
- the skater cannot finish the race due to an injury
- the skater cannot move to the starting line

Tour Skating

Tour skating is another type of skating race. It is a form of long-distance ice-skating racing event. Tour skating is an official skating sport.

This skater is a part of the team skating before him.

Origin

Nordic skating was developed during the 1900s in Sweden from the original Dutch tour skating. Nordic skating is neither known nor practised in the Netherlands. Nordic skating usually involved choosing a set tour over the free ice and moving in groups with all safety equipment on person. Nordic skating is only practised on free and open ice, not in tracks or other artificial ice tracks. Nordic skates differ significantly from the Dutch tour skates.

In Dutch tour skating, skaters follow marked routes on frozen canals and lakes which are coordinated by the Royal Dutch Skating Federation. This is different from Nordic skating, where skaters choose their own routes for the race.

Rules

The rules are similar to other skating competitions. This is a time-based sport. As long as a team reaches together, the winner is announced for the race. In addition to racing each other, skaters are timed for their journey.

The skaters mostly use common skates with long blades. Sometimes they wear speed skates with long blades attached to the skating shoes. Ice-poles and other safety equipment are not carried by them.

In contrast, in Nordic skating, skates are fixed with detachable ice blades as their routes often involve walking between lakes. Elbow and knee pads are often used.

A team of tour skaters are moving along the set path for the race.

Equipment

Ice prods or ice claws are a pair of metal spikes which have handles like sharpened screwdrivers to haul the feet outside the holes in the ice. Ice pikes are a type of pole with metal spikes which have sturdy ski poles to test the thickness of the ice. A tour skater uses a throwing line to pull himself/herself out of the water.

Touring skates with cross-country ski bindings and boots are used by tour skaters. They also use touring skates which have bindings for the hiking boots that they wear. They carry rucksacks with straps for their waist and groin area, so that it stays on without much effort. Tour skaters are asked to carry a change of clothes in their waterproof bags.

Fact card

- Long distance skating in Canada dates back to the period between 1850 and 1900. The skaters used skates with 17-inch long blades. This is said to have enabled them to cover longer distances in shorter time, which was preferable.

Skiing

Skiing is not only an excellent competitive sport, but also a fun recreational activity. Participants use skis to move on the snow. In a skiing race, the aim is to finish faster than any other participant. Skiing is one of the main sports in the Winter Olympics.

A skier is carving a turn down the snowy slope.

Origin

Skiing dates back to almost five millennia. Modern skiing seems to have evolved from Scandinavia. Skiing may have been practised as early as 7000 BCE in what is now known as China. The word "ski" comes from the Old Norse word "skīð" meaning "a stick of wood", which describes the skiing equipment.

Until the mid-nineteenth century, skiing was only seen as a method of transport. After this period, it developed as a sport and activity.

Gameplay

There are three types of skiing:

- **Alpine skiing:** Modern Alpine skiing is divided into the slalom, giant slalom, supergiant slalom (super-G) and downhill events. Super-G and downhill are speed events. The slalom and giant slalom are technical events, where the winners are determined by the lowest combined time.

- **Nordic skiing:** The Nordic or classic skiing sport evolved in the hilly terrain of Norway and other Scandinavian countries. Modern Nordic events are cross country races and ski jumping events.
- **Freestyle skiing:** Freestyle skiing is based on acrobatics. It has three events. These are acro, aerials and moguls. Previously known as "ballet", acro was invented in Europe in the 1930s. In 1924, the International Ski Federation was founded as the world governing body for skiing. They sanctioned the World Championships, which have been held in Nordic events since 1925 for men and 1954 for women. World Championships in Alpine skiing have been held since 1931.

Ski poles are used along with the skis to maintain balance and direct the skis.

Ski boots are bound to the skis with binding gear.

Depending on the level of the skier and the place for skiing, skis have a coating of wax or different textures.

Fact card

- In non-snowy places, a sport called grass skiing replaces regular skiing. Competitors ski on the grassy lawns and slopes rather than on the snow.
- The first Paralympic Winter Games took place in Sweden in 1976. The introduction of sit-ski allowed people in wheelchairs to participate in skiing races.

Skibobbing

Skibobbing, also called "skibiking" or "snowbiking", is a winter sport performed on a vehicle that has the combined features of a bicycle, bobsled and skis. Skibobbing is, thus, sometimes considered a hybrid sport.

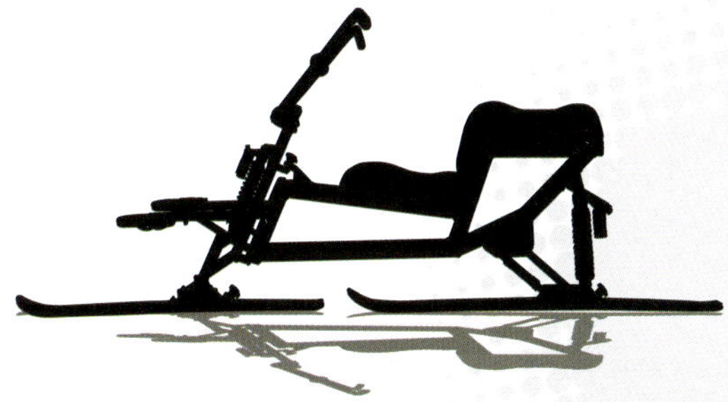

Origin

The first device resembling a skibob was patented in the USA in 1892. There was a similar Austrian device displayed in 1902. The device was originally used by Swiss mailmen and delivery boys. However, after World War II, skibobbing developed as a sport. German Georg Gefäller, in the year 1948, created the Gefäller Ei ("Gefäller Egg"), which he named skibob.

The sport gradually gained international status as it spread from Austria to Switzerland, West Germany, France, Italy and Czechoslovakia. It then went from Europe to the USA, Canada and Japan. The first skibobbing race was held in 1954.

This is an earlier version of the skibob which was developed for safety reasons.

Equipment & Gear

- **Skibob:** The skiob is a lightweight equipment. It can be made of wood, aluminium or plastic. As these are light materials, the participant can easily carry the skibob around during a competition.

The length of a skibob is 1.9–2.29 m. It is a vehicle which resembles a bicycle; but instead of wheels, it uses skis.

- **Gear:** Riders wear short skis on their feet. They also wear a helmet. Goggles are optional but recommended.

Skibob events include the downhill, the slalom, the giant slalom and the supergiant slalom (also known as super-G) events. Downhill has a drop of minimum 365 m for women and 600 m for men. The giant slalom has a less severe drop. It uses about 31 gates for the drops.

The sport was originally started so that people having weak knees could alpine ski. They developed strength in their knees with the skis. It was also carried out by physically challenged people. It became a very popular sport with time, attracting even physically able people to participate. The rules are more or less the same as the ones seen in alpine skiing.

Skibobbing can be done as a group event and even as a singles event.

The winners of the skibobbing contest are standing with their equipment. Winners get certificates along with the prize.

Fact card

- The first skibobbing device was patented in the United States in 1892.
- One of the major attractions of this sport is the speed that people attain. They can travel at speeds of 160 kmph or more.

Bobsledding

Bobsledding is a winter sport in which teams of two or four people slide down narrow, twisting, iced tracks in a sled. Bobsled racing is a popular pastime in many countries. It has become a friendly, non-competitive sport.

An indoor bobsledding competition is in progress.

Origin

Bobsledding developed in the 1880s at the ski resorts of the Swiss Alps. It developed from two skeleton sleds, known as "cresta", which were attached together with a board. They also had a steering wheel attached to the front sled.

The sport got its name when competitors adopted the technique of bobbing back and forth inside the sled to increase their speed.

Bobsledding became an internationally recognised sport when the Fēdēration Internationale de Bobsleigh et de Tobogganing (FIBT) was formed in 1923. It was included in the first Olympic Winter Games held in France in 1924.

Bobsledders wear helmets to protect their heads in case of a fall.

Bobsleds are first pushed down the track by holding onto the back.

Gameplay

- **Tracks:** Modern tracks are made of concrete. They are coated with ice. Each track must have at least a single straight section and one labyrinth. This is three turns in quick succession with no straight section in between. Ideally, a modern track should be 1200–1500 m (3937–4921 feet) long and have at least 15 curves.

- **Sleds:** The current model of sleds (or "sleighs") used at the competition level, are made of light metals. They have steel runners and an aerodynamic composite body.

They must be 3.80-m long or 2.70-m long, depending upon how many people sit upon it.

Fact card

- Bobsleds can attain speeds of 93 mph with the reported world record being 125 mph.

- **Team:** Bobsled crews used to contain six or seven people. This number was reduced to two or four in 1930.

The team consists of a pilot and a breakman. There are two pushers in the case of a four-person team. In a non-professional setting, this number can vary according to the number of people available.

At the beginning, the crew works together to push the bobsled for 50 m from the start line. Then, the crew (or individual) jumps onto the bobsled. Over the rest of the course, a sled's speed depends on its weight, aerodynamics, runners and the condition of the ice. It also depends on the skill of the pilot.

In this picture, the person at the back is bobbing while the driver is still. The team bobs in turns. This is a two-person team.

Luge

Luge is a more professional form of sledding. It requires far more skill and is also comparatively more dangerous.

A slider can remove the steel runners from the luge sled.

Origin

From the fifteenth century, luging has been a traditional winter sport in both Austria and Germany. In 1883, the first international sledding competition was held in Davos, Switzerland. The International Sled Sport Festival originated in Dresden, Germany.

Luge was first introduced as an Olympic sport in 1964 with the men's and women's singles and doubles event.

This track has been created artificially. The surface is smooth and neat.

Gear

A slider wears an aerodynamic bodysuit and spiked gloves. This enables the slider to push the ice away from the ice block at the start of the race, thus propelling the slider down the course.

Wearing a helmet is mandatory. Lugers face the elements head-on, with less equipment on their bodies. The sled, called a luge, is essentially made of wood, or fibreglass with wide runners.

The specially designed ice track is such that it allows gravity to increase the speed of the luge. It demands high concentration and attention from the slider. Ice tracks vary in length but typically range between 1000 m and 1300 m (for men), and between 800 m and 1050 m (for women). Speeds can reach up to 140 kmph as competitors navigate the icy turns.

Luge tracks can also be all-natural. They are developed from the roads and paths available along mountain trails. If a luge track claims to be natural, but has an artificially created curve, it is not allowed to be used for competitions. The track should also have a smooth and horizontal surface, which is regularly maintained. The ice should be natural. There is a possibility that the track gets rough with all the breaking and stopping involved in the race. This should be checked before a match.

Even if it is an artificial track, it must meet certain standards. Otherwise, the sliders would face real danger.

A slider, lies horizontally on the sled and moves along a rounded luge track.

Fact card

- German lugers have dominated the competition with a record of winning 75 medals of the 129 medals awarded for it.
- At the start of the race, athletes are given a number on a bib. The athlete whose number is picked first, goes first.
- Before the race all athletes wait in anticipation for the signal that informs them that the track is clear for the race.

Broomball

Broomball is a sport similar to ice hockey. It is a low expense game. The equipment required is minimal. All a player needs is a broom and a ball or puck. Hence, it is a fairly popular impromptu game.

Origin

The origin and history of this game cannot be confirmed, but from what is known, it is believed that broomball originated in Canada in the early 1900s. Since then, it slowly spread to some other countries with similar climatic conditions. This game is played in a hockey rink. It can be an indoor or outdoor sport, depending on the climate.

Broomball was invented when a group of ice hockey players, seeing that they did not have skates, tried to play the game without them. The first recorded game of broomball was played in Toronto, in 1909. The game spread from Canada to the USA.

A broomball game is in progress, with the opposing teams wearing yellow and white.

Equipment

A small ball is hit by the players across the ice with a 'broom'. The so called 'broom' has a wooden or aluminium shaft, with a rubber moulded head that is triangle shaped and resembles a broom. Special rubber-soled shoes are used by the players instead of skates.

Goaltenders wear a full-face cage mask and thicker padding on their legs, chest and shoulders. They wear blockers. However, they must follow the regulations.

Rules

A broomball match is played between two teams consisting of six players (including a goaltender). The objective is to score more goals than the opponent. Goals are scored by hitting the ball into the opponent's net using the broom.

Tactics, rules and plays are similar to those used in sports such as ice hockey.

The game is supervised by two on-ice referees who hand out penalties for those not following rules. There are off-ice regulators who keep score, time and a count of the penalties. There are also goal judges who take a call for dubious goals.

Goaltenders wear full-face helmets to protect their faces from the fast ball.

The brooms used in broomball usually have wooden or aluminum shafts. Aluminum shafts are stronger than wooden ones.

The ball is usually in a bright colour which can easily be spotted on the field.

Fact card

- Broomball is played in many universities, including the Michigan Technological University, Rochester Institute of Technology, University of Chicago and Boston University.
- Originally, an actual corn broom (with the bristles either cut off or covered with tape) was used to play broomball.

MISCELLANEOUS SPORTS

So far, we have looked at a variety of different sports. We know that there are different games played in the air, in water and on land. There are land sports which are played on beaches and some in the snow.

In this encyclopaedia, the games have been categorised according to the equipment they use. The games include bat-and-ball games, strictly ball games, stick-and-ball games and racquet or board games.

How about the sports that do not fit into any of the categories listed above? There are some games that are rather unique and different from all of the sports listed earlier. We can trace back the origins of some of these games to ancient civilisations. Whereas others have been created in the modern age of movement and adventure.

What binds them all together? It is the spirit of sportsmanship and the desire to be proven better than other people on the field. This is no less true for these miscellaneous sports.

Did you know? In a game called "Jianzi", people use their feet to hit the shuttlecock. It focusses on improving one's coordination skills. It is played by both children and adults. This sport is more than 100 years old as it was invented in the fifth century BCE.

Weightlifting

Weightlifting is an Olympic sport. It is also called "Olympic weightlifting". In this sport, an athlete tries to lift a barbell, which is fitted with weights, in one single attempt.

Origin

While the origin of this competition is vague, it is believed that for the longest time there have been competitions to establish who can lift the heaviest weight. Evidences of these competitions have been found in Egypt, China and ancient Greece. However, the Olympic weightlifting sport can be traced back to the nineteenth century when the European competitions were held.

The first Olympic Games, which took place in 1896, had a weightlifting round as a part of the field events. Today, it is a part of the Track and Field or Athletics event. Though absent in the 1900 Olympic Games, it made a comeback in 1904.

There are two competition lifts which have been defined for the Olympics. These are the "snatch" and the "clean and jerk".

During a snatch, the weightlifter lifts the barbell from the ground and brings it overhead in one movement.

In the clean and jerk move, there are two steps. The "clean" move has the weightlifter moving the barbell from the floor to a racked position across deltoids and clavicles. During the "jerk" move, the weightlifter raises the barbell and keeps it still above the head.

In these moves, the judges look for the proper form and also note down any hesitation or shaking that the weightlifter might experience.

Rules

Weightlifting has always been an individual sport. It has been refined by different training and age group categories. Weightlifting has a high incidence of injury and thus the training for this sport is strictly monitored. It has both male and female categories.

The World Weightlifting Federation (WWF) proposed the rules of this game in the twentieth century. The commonly accepted rules are:

1. Olympic weightlifters can only perform the snatch and clean and jerk moves and no other form of weightlifting.
2. Each weightlifter gets three attempts to make these lifts. The combined score of the two highest scored attempts is the overall result and determines if the weightlifter has won or lost the game.
3. No parts of the lifter should touch the platform.
4. If a lifter fails to complete a successful snatch move and a clean and jerk move for whatever reasons, he/she will not be given a total score. Their entry in the weightlifting competition is considered incomplete.

Smaller dumbells are used to practice weightlifting and to build arm strength.

The elbow must be bent in such a way that the arm forms an L shape.

Two or more weights can be added to a barbell. There is a fix which needs to be placed to keep the weights in place.

Weightlifting competitions test the explosive strength of the body. The lifts are expected to be carried out faster, with flexibility, range and mobility. If done properly, a weightlifting move looks very graceful to the observer, even at the slowest speed.

Weightlifters build their upper body and core strength with an exercise called "arm curls". In this exercise, they repeatedly raise the barbell loaded with weights up and down, with their fingers firmly curling around it.

Wall of fame

Henri Gance was a French weightlifter who won the gold medal at the 1920 Summer Olympics which happened in Antwerp.

Carlo Galimberti, an Italian weightlifter, won the gold medal in the 1924 Olympic Games in Paris.

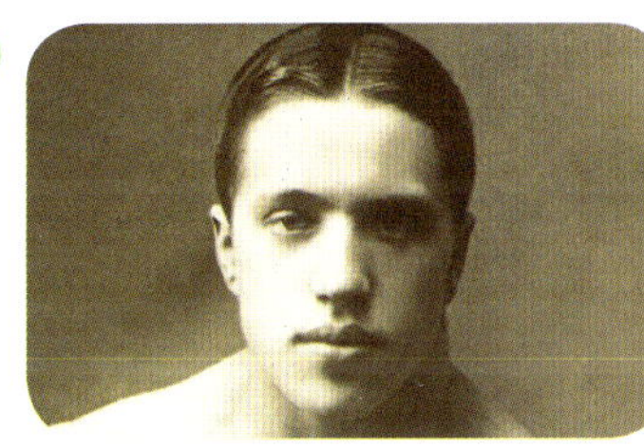

Alfred Neuland won a gold medal at the 1920 Summer Olympics in Antwerp.

Fact card

- The stronger a weightlifter's muscles, the faster they will contract. This is actually not good for the competition level as the weightlifter will then perform the move very slowly.
- Though weightlifting is an energetic game, it adds to the overall size of the weightlifter. The waist, arms and legs actually "bulk up" with muscle and fat.
- The weightlifter who lifts the heaviest weight is given a prize. The competitor who choose to lift the lowest weight, goes first.

Roller Derby

Roller derby is a "female-only" contact race sport that involves a lot of offense and defence actions. Roller derby is a skating game and is played indoors. However, some versions of it can be played outdoors.

Origin

The game was invented in the mid-1880s. It was included in the multi-day endurance event with the aim that the winner would be awarded a cash prize at the end. The techniques used in the game, as well as the firm movements and spins executed by the skaters, won it a large fanbase. By 1930, the current and contemporary form of the sport was developed. The rules were changed and more body contact was allowed. Soon enough, the game transformed into a team event as seen today. The system of point scoring and completing laps came into order.

For the competition level, roller derby players need to tie up their hair.

Roller derby players wear knee-length socks or fishnet stockings.

Gameplay

Roller derby has 14 players in two teams. The teams are further divided into five players per jam. They simultaneously skate on the track in a counterclockwise manner. Each team designates a scoring player or a "jammer" while the other four players are designated as "the blockers". There is a provision when a blocker can become the jammer. The blocker and the jammer have different helmets, while the others have open helmets.

The bout is played for 60 minutes each. Points are scored upon completing laps before the opponent. Blockers use body contact to protect their own jammers and prevent the other team from doing so.

A team showing off its skates and socks. Style and coordination are important parts of the roller derby.

Fact card

- Team members need to think of a team name and also a "skater name".
- The bouts are given fun and creative names. "Night of the rolling dead" is one such name.

Tug of War

There are several games which completely depend upon sheer individual strength. However, many martial sports emphasised the development of team strength over individual strength. The most popular game in the latter category is the tug of war.

Origin

The tug of war has a mythological origin. According to the mythological stories, this game was played between the Sun and the Moon for lightness and darkness. The first record of human beings ever involving themselves in this sport was made in Egypt, Greece and China.

According to the old Tang dynasty, "Notes of Feng" or "tug of war" developed from the practice of hook pulling. At the time, the king had encouraged 1000 of his subjects to carry out a tug of war, with 500 people on each side of the long rope. He brought in drummers to motivate his own team. Ancient Indians saw this game as a way of settling disputes. It was a part of the Olympic Games until 1920.

An old painting in a temple showing the tug of war game in progress.

Rules

In1920, along with 33 other sports, tug of war was removed from the Olympic Games. Since then several countries have set up their own tug of war associations. Tug of War International Federation (TWIF) began in 1960. Today, it is a well-flourished sport and has celebrities playing it as well. There are some strict rules to follow at the competition levels.

This game is played between two teams. There should be at least eight people in one team.

Tug of war is usually played as a team building sport in corporations.

The rope is marked in the centre with a ribbon. There are lines made to mark the end zones and the pull zones. A team member sitting or falling down during the play is immediately removed.

Even a player pushing his/her elbow below the knee level is given a foul point. This process is called "locking".

The rope must be pulled with it under the arm. There are no exceptions to be allowed for this rule. Sometimes the game rules are modified depending on the circumstances but the basic rules never change.

A group of friends playing the tug of war game.

Fact card

- A combined team of members from Sweden and Denmark won the first Olympic gold medal in tug of war. In the finals, they had defeated France.
- It was believed that the Gods and the demons played the tug of war game between themselves.

Footbag

A "footbag" is a small, round, ball-like bag which is used to play different kinds of sports. Footbag is a variation of football as in this sport, the player kicks a ball repeatedly and it focusses on the display of skills. It is also a score-oriented game.

Origin

The modern version of footbag was invented in the USA in 1972. It was called "hacky sack" at the time. The competitive version of the game began in 1978, and it was called footbag net. Various types and styles of playing this game have been developed. Freestyling is the most common and highly followed one.

Equipment

For this sport, the players use a crocheted footbag filled with plastic beads. There are other variations of this where instead of beads, the ball is filled with sand or dirt. They are named "sand hacks" or "dirt bags" accordingly.

While sand hacks are good for beginners who are still learning the sport, crocheted footbags with plastic pebbles are good for those who are going for competitions.

Footbags are beautiful and colourful in appearance as they are crocheted.

Rules

The player makes a combination of moves and stunts with the bag. The last move of the last trick is the first move of the next trick. In this sport, players need to jump, flip their feet and perform several other athletic moves with their feet and legs. This sport develops the calf muscles of the legs.

Players can use a footbag instead of a ball in various other games played with a net as the goal. A racquet is used to hit the bag and push it into a goal net. Circle kick is another variation of the footbag games.

In circle kick, people stand in a circle and prevent the bag from falling onto the ground. The other forms of footbag games are Bruce, Footbag golf, Horse, Kickback, Knockout, Number catch, Numbers, Shark and War.

Not all of these games are played at the professional level. These games have been developed by fans of the sport. They play the variations and then spread it around.

There have been world records for the number of times a person has managed to kick the footbag without dropping it. A man named Ted Martin has managed to keep a game of footbag going for over eight hours, with a total of 63,326 kicks.

He made this record on June 14, 1997 during a Classic Footbag event in Chicago, Illinois, USA.

A man performs a footbag trick during an official event.

Fact card

- This game has more than 10 variations which can be incorporated in most of the other sports as well.
- A game variation called "horse" helps improve the freestyle method, which is yet another variation in the sport of footbag.

Foosball

Foosball is also called "table football". Foosball is a popular indoor recreational sport, especially amongst college students in the USA, UK and Germany.

Just like football, the foosball match starts at the centre circle.

The ball is a miniature version of a real football.

Origin

Its origin is unknown, but the mention of this game was made back in 1920. Foosball was created when an English football club supporter asked for a miniature game of football that he could play at home. Soon, the foosball table was taken to another country and patented there. Later, in 2002, the International Table Soccer Federation (ITSF) was formed. This game keeps undergoing several reforms but the basic rules remain the same.

Rules

The game begins when the ball is served through a hole that is on one side of the table. The ball can also be placed on the table manually. There are figures mounted on the rotating bars that can be held by the player. The players thus rotate the bars and move the mounted players to play the game.

In certain conditions, the 360° shot is not allowed (where the foosball players rotate 360°). It is considered an illegal move. The Federation has made sure that the rules are kept the same for all the games. The table usually has eight rows of "foosball men". They could be made of any material, but are usually made of plastic or wood. Each team has one or two human players who control the rotating rods accordingly.

Foosball is popular with the younger generation, especially among college students.

Players rotate the handles. Each player occupies one side of the table.

The foosemen stay in the same rod and cannot be moved. They wear different uniforms.

The foosball table is placed on diagonal wooden stands.

Fact card

- In this game, the ball can travel across the table at a speed of 56 kmph.
- The game has been played in television shows and movies. A popular TV show named *Friends* has frequently shown a foosball table.

Cheerleading

Cheerleading is a sport that started off as a routine to improve the morale of the players of a team. Today, it has become a competitive sport all on its own.

Cheerleading is taught in high schools and colleges in North America.

Origin

Cheerleading started in the 1860s, and originated in England when a set of fans were hooting, shouting and dancing to support their team.

The cheerleading movement first started as an all-male sport. In 1923, women from the University of Minnesota participated in the sport.

By the 1970s, women had started cheering in public events to support their teams. Since 1973, the sport has been dominated by women, with nearly 95 per cent of the world's cheerleaders being women. Cheerleaders were enlisted to raise the morale of basketball and later football players.

Cheerleaders use shiny and colourful "pom poms" for their routines.

All cheerleading groups assign a captain.

The captain, along with a trained choreographer, trains the rest of the group.

Cheerleading teams also have vice captains who manage the teams.

Cheerleaders wear bright coloured outfits and perform choreographed moves.

Organisations

There are various types of teams in this sport. The teams are categorised on the basis of age. The major types are school-sponsored, middle school, high school, youth league athletic associations, All-Star and also the professional level cheerleading groups.

There are various organisations like the Americheer, International Cheer Union, International Federation of Cheerleading, National Cheerleaders Association, United Spirit Association, Universal Cheerleaders Association and others who provide both training as well as a professional platform to cheerleaders.

Each cheerleading team is customised for the performances. Different age groups are judged on different criteria, as well as on the skill level.

It is believed that the sport of cheerleading requires the strength of a footballer, the grace of a dancer and dynamic gymnastic abilities.

The competition aspect keeps on changing and hence brings new routines into the picture.

Most teams have to have a professional choreographer to ensure that the act is best showcased within the rules. These teams need to wear the same set of uniforms to show both uniformity and unity. Popular teams are identified by the colour of their uniforms.

There are several reports of injuries in this sport. The competitions have strict safety rules in place to avoid injuries and accidents. The acts are performed mostly in an indoor setup but occasionally they are held outside as well. Certain competitions also allow a combination of all age groups and both sexes to take part as a team. This creates a bridge between both levels of skills and gives a chance for new acts to come up.

The major competitions are Asia Thailand Cheerleading, Cheerleading Asia Open, Cheerleading World Championships, ICU World Championships, National Cheerleading Championships, etc.

All cheerleading routines have a strict time limit. Each round in a professional competition usually lasts for two minutes and 30 seconds. Performances are judged on the expression, teamwork, enthusiasm, energy and other factors that make the act lively. In co-ed performances, the male cheerleaders showcase their strength by using lift and roll techniques.

Professional cheerleaders perform for the NBA and the NFL games. These organisations also hold contests to identify potential cheerleaders for their teams.

Wall of fame

Paula Abdul, a very famous singer and choreographer, began her career as a cheerleader for the Los Angeles Lakers at the age of 18.

American actress Ali Landry was the captain of her high school cheerleaders club.

The 40th President of the USA, Ronald Reagan, was a cheerleader at the Eureka College, where he studied.

Fact card

- Cheerleading was considered to be one of the most dangerous school activities in the early 2000s.
- This sport is played at all levels, right from high school to professional level.
- In the USA, of the entire student body across all the universities and schools, only three per cent are involved in cheerleading. But they account for nearly 65 per cent of all injuries in girls' health and school athletics sports.

Speed Cubing

Speed cubing involves the solving of a Rubik's cube in the least possible time.

Origin

Erno Rubik was a Hungarian professor who invented the Rubik's cube in 1974. In 1980, the game turned into a worldwide craze and gained popularity very fast.

The game attained popularity so quickly that a world competition was held in 1982 in Hungary. Later on, the craze for Rubik's cube started dying off due to the monotony of the player's attempt to do the same thing over and over again. However soon, new cubes came into existence and online communities were formed, which led to a further increase in the demand.

There were multiple solutions to the problem. The extra dimensions allowed the player to keep brainstorming for a longer time. Now, there is a totally new wave of speed cubing that has come into existence.

The players have to get all the cubes of the same colour on one face.

Each row and column of the cube can be twisted around.

Gameplay

There are various ways of solving the puzzle and the competitions are based on a timer. The player is free to choose his/her approach to solve the puzzle. The various methods of solving the puzzle are CFOP method, ROUX method, ZZ method, Petrus method and Corners-first method. According to the World Cube Association, there are only a limited set of moves within which the player can solve the cube.

The corners-first method is an easy beginner method where the player first solves the corners, then solves the edges with slice turns, and then solves the middle portion of the cube.

There is a typical "stackmat" timer that is used in this game to measure the time. The player is supposed to place his palms on the mat board. This resets the timer to zero. Once the player lifts his hands, the timer sets off and the player has to solve the cube as fast as possible. In this process, he/she can use any technique that fits best to him/her. Once the cube is solved, he/she does not have to place the cube down properly, but can simply drop the cube.

The sensors detect touch on the pad and stop the timer. This enables the judge to check the timing in microseconds. This being a cut-throat competitive game, accuracy in judgment is very essential.

The game is based on various types of cubes or puzzles. These basically determine the rules of the game. The rule of being the fastest remains the same in most of them.

There are various records set for age bars as well. A player's capability at a particular age is no longer a criteria for judging.

The various categories include speed solving, blindfolded solving, multiple blindfolded solving, one hand solving, solving with feet and solving in fewest moves. The complexity of the problem would determine the kind of approach. There are world competitions held in each category and each method of the game.

The contestants are competing in a timed event. Their time is being displayed on the LED screen on their desk before them.

Certain competitions also have no age bar and are judged on absolute level.

The various types of cubes that are used in these competitions are 2 x 2, 3 x 3, 4 x 4, 5 x 5, 6 x 6 and 7 x 7.

There are other puzzles that run on the same timer principle. They also fall under the speed cubing game. They are Megaminx, Pyraminx, Square, Rubik's clock and Skewb.

Players also have the option of using lubrication so that the movement of the cube becomes faster and easier. Other ways are to set a cube in a certain pattern prior to placing hands on the timer mats.

The megaminx is a dodecahedron-shaped puzzle. It has about 50 pieces which can be moved and it is much more complex than the 20-piece Rubik's Cube.

This is the pyramix. It is a regular tetrahedron puzzle which has the format of the Rubik's Cube.

The Square One can change shape as and when it is twisted because it is cut in a special way.

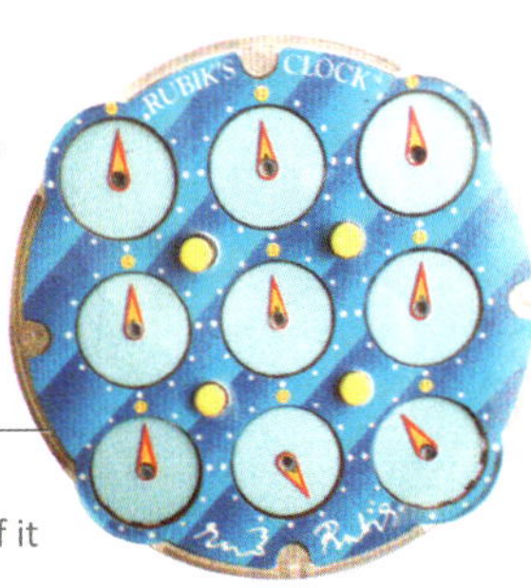

This is the Rubik's Clock. Each side of it has nine clocks.

This is a skewb. It was a part of the Pyraminx series.

Wall of fame

Felix Zemdegs solved the Rubik's Cube in 7.36 seconds in 2013.

Michal Pleskowicz held the record for solving the Rubik's Cube in 8.65 seconds. He did this in 2011.

Breanden Vallance holds a record of 10.74 seconds in solving the Rubik's Cube. He holds the third rank in the World's Greatest Players list.

Fact card

- There are 43 quintillion ways to solve a Rubik's Cube.
- If you would turn a Rubik's Cube once every second, it would take you 1400 trillion years to go through all permutations.
- The Rubik's Cube is the best-selling toy of all time.
- Only 20 pieces of the Rubik's Cube can be moved. But the other variations of the cube can be moved several times.
- The four tips of the pyramix can be rotated very easily. The rest of the colours need to line up to them.

Baton Twirling

Baton twirling is a sport which requires the manipulation of a baton in a graceful and co-ordinated manner.

Origin

The development of baton twirling can be traced back to Eastern Europe and Asia. According to some, it started at dance festivals. Initially, these practitioners used knives, rifles, torches and sticks to twirl with and toss.

These traditions then passed into the armies of some countries that often twirled with rifles during marches.

During parades, there was a rifle twirler at the front of the march. The rifle was replaced with a "mace". The mace had a heavy head. As a result, it was unbalanced at one end. It was also much larger than the batons that are used today.

The involvement of women (called "drum majorettes") who used the batons for their routines, led to modifications in the design of the mace. This was also due to the fact that twirling had become more frequent with them. They now resembled batons. These batons were made from hollow light metal, balanced and given symmetrical ends of light rubber.

In this sport, the participant needs to coordinate properly and have extraordinary control of the body. The participant also needs to be flexible in order to execute the many acrobatic and rhythmic movements involved in the competition. New or young learners of this routine usually practice with small elbow twirls and work their way up to harder routines.

Today, many member countries have their own national organisations. At a global level, the World Baton Twirling Federation (WBTF), the World Twirling Association (WTA), and The Global Alliance of National Baton Twirling and Majorette Associations (NBTA) are the three recognised governing bodies of baton twirling.

The United States Twirling Association, Incorporated, hosted the first World Championships in Seattle, Washington in 1980 with great popularity.

Subsequently, one member country of the WBTF holds the championship each year in August.

Gameplay

The baton twirling competition is divided into different events based on the age group of the participants.

These categories are junior, senior and adult for both men and women. Modern competitions also have participation by individuals, state teams, educational institutions and recreational groups of any age or gender.

There are different competitions, such as single, double, triple and multiple baton twirling. Most baton twirling competitions involve a routine set to music or a rhythm. These routines consist of a set of compulsory elements, moves and routines.

Baton twirling is a very important part of marching routines. The marching band walks behind the baton twirler who leads the way.

The compulsory routines are a showcase of skills for apple-to-apple comparison between athletes. The optional (freestyle) part is a platform for them to showcase their creativity through their routine.

Countries like France, Japan, Italy and the USA have consistently dominated world championship competitions since the time of its conception. There are freestyle rounds for men and women. There must be a short programme for all events like struts, dance twirls, pairs, trios, show choirs, one baton, two baton, three baton, teams and groups.

The artistic twirl rounds were introduced in the freestyle and dance twirl categories at the International Cup. One of the most important events in the baton twirling field is the "Twirl Mania" which is hosted by the ESPN Wide World of Sports in Disneyland. It is a unique celebration of the baton twirling sport.

Teams, high schools, universities and solo groups participate in baton twirling rounds. Competitors march in the opening march ceremony in clothes that represent the groups and schools they come from.

Wall of fame

The World Baton Twirling Federation met at Paris, France in 1979 to finalise plans for the World Championships of Baton Twirling.

The World Baton Twirling Federation held the first World Championships in Washington.

Italy is one of the most prominent members of the World Baton Twirling Federation.

Fact card

- Some marching bands at parades still use maces for twirling. The macebearer or "drum major" twirls this mace at the front of the parade.
- ESPN Wide World of Sports' show, Twirl Mania in Walt Disney World is an annual event. It is a recreational competition for gymnasts and dancers from sports like baton twirling, cheerleading, dancing and so on. It gives a platform to young enthusiasts of the fields.

Unicycle Hockey

Unicycle hockey is a fairly self-explanatory sport. The game involves the use of unicycles instead of one's feet. It gets ten times tougher when you factor in the slippery floors of the arena.

Origin

Unicycle hockey was first referenced in a German silent movie named "Variete". It was released in 1925. Though they did not depict it, they had referenced it in actions. In the Bicycle Journal, there was a report of the Albuquerque Unicycle Club of the USA playing hockey on the unicycle. This took place in 1960. In 1962, the Columbia Unicycles Federation had suggested the game in their pamphlets.

Fact card

- A player might only partake in the game while riding a unicycle. If they fall, they have to mount at the same spot as the fall.
- Only five per cent of the total world players are female.

Gameplay

The game is very similar to the original game of hockey but with unicycles.

A tennis ball is used with either a hockey stick or an ice hockey stick. The court size differs as per the game, but is usually 40 m in length and 25-m wide.

One of the biggest differences between regular hockey and unicycle hockey is that the nets are placed slightly forward. This allows the players to even continue the game behind the net.

This sport can be played in all sorts of indoor courts, parking lots, tennis courts or other places with smooth, flat grounds. The goalies have a bigger wheeled unicycle than the others. The others use a small-diameter wheel in order to turn quickly and acquire greater speed.

The International Unicycling Hockey Federation sets the rules for competitions. More than 16 countries participate in this contest. Each team consists of five players and also substitutes. There is no fixed goalie player unlike in field hockey. However, one or the other player usually takes up this role. After each goal, players move to their own half.